Meditation Mandalas: Messages From the Star Horses

Coloring Book

Regyna Curtis | Dawn Phoenix

Copyright © 2021 Regyna Curtis | Dawn Phoenix

All Rights Reserved

www.atmaitri.com | www.dawnphoenix.org

Table of Contents

1. Our Story: The Star Horses of Corolla 1
2. Star Horses 2
3. Accuracy 4
4. Animal Guide 6
5. Being-ness 8
6. Childhood 10
7. Compromise 12
8. Creation 14
9. Distraction 16
10. Divine Self Remembrance 18
11. Dreams 20
12. Faith 22
13. Friendship 24
14. Gaia's Sacred Womb 26
15. Intention 28
16. Invitation 30
17. Learning 32
18. Listening 34
19. Love 36
20. Music 38
21. Music of the Stars 40
22. New Horizons 42
23. Non-Verbal Communication 44
24. Partnership 46
25. Reconnect with Nature 48

26.	Service	50
27.	Share	52
28.	Simplicity	54
29.	Story	56
30.	Telepathic Communication	58
31.	The High Mind	60
32.	Transformation	62
33.	Travel	64
34.	Truth	66
35.	Variety	68
About Regyna		70
About Dawn		71

Our Story: The Star Horses of Corolla

For the first time ever, the enigmatic "wild Spanish Mustangs" living on the beaches of Corolla, North Carolina reveal their secrets in The Star Horses of Corolla. Where did they REALLY come from? Why are they here? What can we learn from them? Certified Animal Communicator Dawn Phoenix's interview with the lead stallion, Jacko is the basis for this true story. Speaking directly to children, Jacko's messages of wisdom, inspiration, and the horses' love for humanity will inspire young and old alike. Children are our planet's future caregivers, and the Star Horses support them with easy ways to stay anchored in love, light, and peace in a chaotic world.

Now the Star Horses return to support you on your journey through the combination of creativity and contemplation. Each page in this coloring book is infused with a message shared by the Star Horses and transformed into meditative mandalas by Art Channel, Regyna Curtis.

This collaboration comes from a place of love to support you, bring you joy, and remind you that all humans benefit from taking time to play and create. May you find just that in the pages of our book.

STAR HORSES

WISDOM FROM THE STAR HORSES TO CONTEMPLATE AS YOU CREATE.

ACCURACY

PAY SPECIAL ATTENTION TO THE DETAILS IN YOUR LIFE. IT'S EASY TO OVERLOOK SOMETHING IMPORTANT IF IT'S HIDDEN WITHIN OTHER INFORMATION.

Animal Guide

There may be an animal guide communicating something important to you. Listen for these messages with your heart.

BEING-NESS

TAKE TIME TO JUST BE. SIT IN STILLNESS AND JUST BREATHE. HOW DOES IT FEEL?

CHILDHOOD

TAKE TIME OUT TO BE LIKE A CHILD. ALLOW YOUR INNER CHILD TO TAKE OVER FOR A WHILE AND SEE HOW GOOD IT FEELS!

COMPROMISE

IS THERE AN AREA IN YOUR LIFE YOU CAN PRACTICE COMPROMISE WITHOUT SACRIFICING YOUR HAPPINESS OR INTEGRITY?

CREATION

REMEMBER YOUR CREATIVE POWER. CREATE WHAT YOU DESIRE, NOT THE THINGS YOU'RE AFRAID OF OR DO NOT WANT.

DISTRACTION

WHAT'S DISTRACTING YOU FROM HEARING YOUR INNER GUIDANCE? TECHNOLOGY? PEOPLE?

DIVINE SELF REMEMBRANCE

WHAT IN YOUR LIFE IS CALLING YOU TO REMEMBER YOUR TRUE DIVINE NATURE?

DREAMS

PAY SPECIAL ATTENTION TO YOUR DREAMS WHEN YOU SLEEP. THE UNIVERSE IS ALWAYS COMMUNICATING WITH YOU.

FAITH

HAVE FAITH IN YOURSELF. THERE IS NOTHING YOU CANNOT DO.

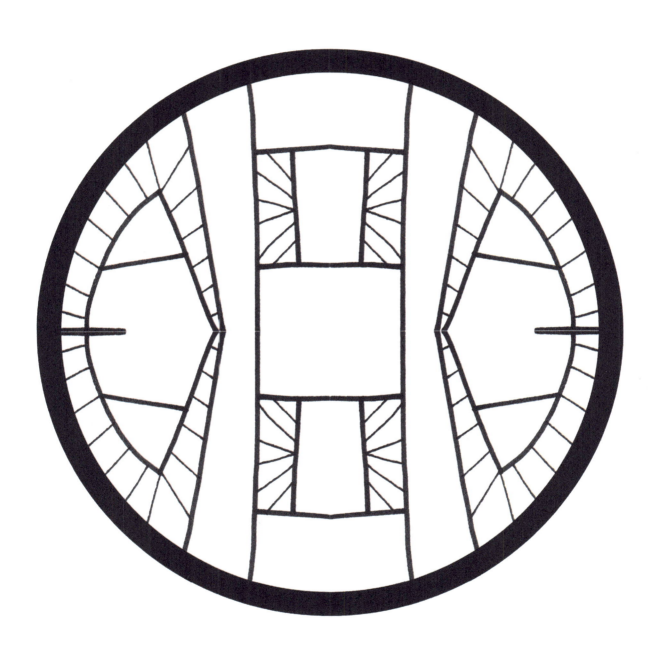

FRIENDSHIP

BE SURE YOU ARE ATTENTIVE TO YOUR FRIENDS. IS THERE SOMEONE WHO COULD USE YOUR SUPPORT?

GAIA'S SACRED WOMB

KNOW THAT DURING THIS TIME OF CHANGE, YOU RESIDE IN GAIA'S SACRED WOMB. SHE FACILITATES THIS TRANSITION WITH EASE AND GRACE.

INTENTION

THE MORE YOU SET INTENTIONS, THE EASIER IT WILL GET. EVENTUALLY, EVERYTHING THAT HAPPENS TO YOU WILL BE INTENTIONAL.

INVITATION

If you receive an invitation to do something you don't usually do, it may be in your highest good to accept it. Growth comes from stepping outside of your comfort zone.

LEARNING

BE OPEN TO NEW INFORMATION. IT CAN COME IN MANY FORMS, SO PAY ATTENTION!

LISTENING

PAY ATTENTION WHEN OTHERS SPEAK. THE UNIVERSE MAY BE SPEAKING THROUGH THEM WITH MORE THAN THE WORDS YOU HEAR.

LOVE

REMEMBER AS YOU SHOW OTHERS LOVE TO SHOW YOURSELF SOME LOVE, TOO.

MUSIC

SINGING, PLAYING AN INSTRUMENT, OR LISTENING TO MUSIC ARE ALL WAYS TO CONNECT TO THE UNIVERSE AND RECEIVE MESSAGES.

MUSIC OF THE STARS

WHAT ARE THEIR SONGS TELLING YOU? CAN YOU QUIET YOUR MIND AND BODY LONG ENOUGH TO HEAR THE MESSAGES IN THEIR MELODIES?

NEW HORIZONS

WHAT NEW IDEA, PROJECT, OR ENDEAVOR CAN YOU START?

Non-Verbal Communication

Pay close attention to the body language of others. There is much communicated without words.

PARTNERSHIP

FOCUS ON BUILDING RELATIONSHIPS THAT BENEFIT EVERYONE INVOLVED.

RECONNECT WITH NATURE

What are ways you can reconnect with nature? You could walk on the beach, put a house plant in your workspace, sit in a field, or go for a hike on a trail.

SERVICE

HOW CAN YOU BE OF SERVICE TO THE GREATER GOOD? CAN YOU DO ANYTHING TO SUPPORT ANOTHER ON THEIR PATH?

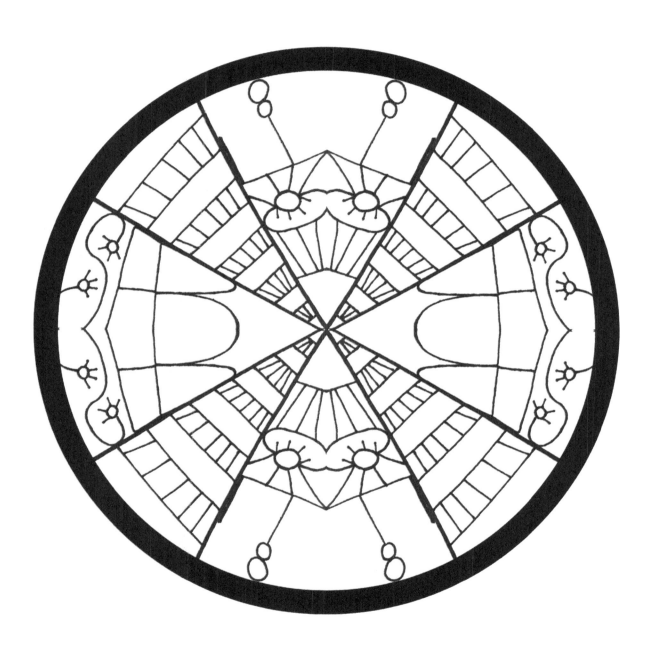

SHARE

WHAT DO YOU HAVE AN ABUNDANCE OF THAT YOU CAN SHARE WITH OTHERS?

SIMPLICITY

WHAT CAN YOU AFFORD TO SPEND LESS TIME DOING? WHAT WILL SIMPLIFY YOUR LIFE IF YOU LET IT GO?

Story

What loving wisdom can you impart to someone who could benefit from it? You can use a story to get the information across in a fun way, if necessary.

Telepathic Communication

Tune into the people, plants, and animals around you to receive messages. What do you taste, hear, feel, or smell?

THE HIGH MIND

WHAT DO YOU NEED TO SEE FROM A HIGHER PERSPECTIVE?

Transformation

Be aware of changes within or around you. They may mark an important turning point.

MEDITATION MANDALAS: MESSAGES FROM THE STAR HORSES

TRAVEL

Is there somewhere you have been wanting to visit? Travel can mean more than driving and flying from one place to another.

TRUTH

TUNE INTO YOUR BODY TO FEEL WHAT RESONATES WITHIN YOU AS TRUTH AND WHAT DOES NOT. THE TRUTH SHOULD ALWAYS FEEL GOOD.

Variety

Acknowledge the differences that make you unique. Variety should be celebrated!

About Regyna

Art Channel, Soul Wisdom Mentor, Author, Speaker

Regyna Curtis is an international bestselling author on the subjects of spirituality and creativity. Her stories take you on an adventure of self-discovery, weaving insights from her personal journey throughout the physical and spiritual realms with her work as a Soul Wisdom Mentor.

With over 40 years of experience living as an intuitive being, Regyna has achieved fluency in the language of her soul. She is an expert in interpreting soul wisdom languages and uses this to support and empower individuals in finding confidence and clarity to live their most authentically soul-aligned lives.

A natural storyteller with a gift for relaying complex concepts in relatable, useful, and entertaining ways, Regyna will keep you on the edge of your seat, curious to know what happens next. She is a sought-after speaker and workshop facilitator, the founder of her soul-led business Atmaitri, an art channel, and an enthusiastic world traveler.

Website: www.atmaitri.com

Soul Wisdom Artwork: www.etsy.com/shop/atmaitri

Soul Wisdom Quiz: www.atmaitri.com/quiz

Want to work with me? https://calendly.com/atmaitri/soul-wisdom-mentoring-exploration

Social Media: @Atmaitri on Instagram, Facebook, YouTube

LinkedIn: www.linkedin.com/in/regyna-curtis-1472b47/

Linktr.ee: https://linktr.ee/Atmaitri

About Dawn

Channel, Author, Energy Healer

Dawn Phoenix is a Certified Clinical Hypnotherapist (C.C.H.t) and holds a Master of Teaching (M.T.). She is a Certified Dolphin Energy Healing Practitioner, Certified Animal Communicator, Channel, and international best-selling author.

She is also a former elementary school teacher. Bringing her love of children together with her Animal Communication skills in 2020, she wrote The Star Horses of Corolla, an empowering children's book told from the perspective of a group of very unique horses living on the beaches of Corolla, North Carolina.

Dawn works with people to help them release that which no longer serves them, reclaim their power as the true creators of their reality, and transform into who they were originally divinely designed to be.

Website: https://www.dawnphoenix.org

Explore more of my books: https://www.dawnphoenix.org/shop

Book Online: https://www.dawnphoenix.org/book-online

Connect with me:

Loom of Tales App (free): https://loomoftales.app/dawn-phoenix-invites-you

Facebook: https://www.facebook.com/dawnphoenixtransformationalhealer

Email: dawn@dawnphoenix.org

Made in the USA
Columbia, SC
30 December 2022

74113063R10043